The Fall of the Roman Empire

The Fall of the Roman Empire

Empire

How to Mismanage an Empire

By: A.C. Dunne

Witty History A Division of Epocto Labs

Copyright

Publisher Information
Published by Epocto Labs LLC Epoctolabs@gmail.com

Welcome Gift

Have you ever been trapped at a party by Bob, the World's Most Boring Historian, droning on about crop rotation in the Middle Ages with the enthusiasm of a sloth on tranquilizers? Imagine a lively character steps in, shoves Bob aside, and re-spins the tale so you're rolling with laughter.

Meet Witty History. We're that lively character, and your dry history textbook is Bob. We pride ourselves on our ability to trip lightly over the cobblestones of time while pushing Bob out of the way, making history delightful instead of daunting. And our plan is ingeniously simple: tell history in a different way.

Here's your golden ticket: **www.wittyhistory.com**. This isn't your average webpage—it's a gateway to a world where history laughs, jokes, and keeps you hooked. We're so committed to making history enjoyable that we're offering you a **FREE EBOOK** that's entertaining and eye-opening.

You will love **MYSTERIES AND UNSOLVED EVENTS: History Loves a Good Cliffhanger.**

Just enter your email, and this riveting book is all yours. Plus, you'll always be first in line for our newest witty tales. But act fast! You don't want to be left behind in the dust of the past, do you?

Otherwise, it's back to Bob and his monotone monologues. So why suffer? **Claim your free eBook**, sign up for the laughs, and let Witty History inject humor into your historical knowledge.

To my grandmother Darleen,

Whose quiet grace and boundless affection profoundly shaped my world.

TABLE OF CONTENTS

— CHAPTER 1 —

YOUR INDUCTION
INTO ROME'S EXCESSIVE DRAMA

Why Bother with Rome's Downfall?

So, you've chosen to take a journey with us through the fall of Rome - a time when toga parties were all the rage, "tweeting" was something only birds did, and "Romeflix and chill" meant a day at the Colosseum. But why should we venture back to a time long before WiFi and reality T.V.? We're about to dive into the nitty-gritty of it.

First things first, let's talk about size and influence. The Roman Empire was big - like, huge. It was the kind of big that makes your favorite celebrity's mansion look like a Barbie dollhouse. It stretched from the sandy dunes of Africa to the rolling hills of northern England and from the sunny coasts of Spain to the fertile plains of Mesopotamia. If the Roman Empire was a game of Monopoly, it would have hotels on pretty much every property.

And let's remember how long it lasted. Over a thousand years! That's older than your grandma's grandma's...well, you get the point. It's old. And during that time, the Romans achieved things that would make even Bill Gates envious. They gave us the blueprint for modern government, developed a legal system that's still partly in use today and built architectural wonders that have stood the test of time.

But let's cut to the chase. What's so fascinating about Rome's fall? Why not focus on its rise or its heyday? Well, for starters, drama is always more interesting. And the fall of Rome had more drama than a soap opera - power struggles, invasions, economic crises, the works.

On a more serious note, studying the fall of Rome offers a treasure trove of lessons. It's like an ancient instruction manual titled 'What Not to Do When You're Running an Empire.' Political corruption? Check. Economic instability? You bet. Overexpansion? They wrote the book on it. It's as if Rome could predict the future, predicting challenges we still face in today's world.

And let's not forget about the people. The fall of Rome wasn't just an event but a human experience. By studying it, we get a glimpse into how people reacted, adapted, and, ultimately, survived. It's a testament to human resilience in the face of change.

So, as we embark on this journey back in time, remember: we're not just doing it for the gladiators and the grapes. We're exploring the fall of Rome to learn, understand, and, of course, appreciate the drama. It's like a Roman once said, "Historia est magistra vitae" - "History is life's teacher." I mean, nowadays, it seems like no one is listening to that teacher but instead watching TikTok during class, but you get the point.

What to Expect from This Book

So, you're about to embark on a whirlwind tour of Rome's glorious rise and dramatic fall. But what exactly are you signing up for? Well, think of this book as your personal Delorean (the time-traveling car from "Back to the Future," in case you missed that reference), ready to transport you back to the days of gladiators, emperors, and really uncomfortable sandals.

We're going to explore the Roman Empire in all its glory, from its most grandiose triumphs to its epic fails. We'll delve into the juicy bits of political intrigue, the barbarian invasions (spoiler alert: it's not all about the barbarians), and even the surprising rise of the religion, Christianity.

This isn't your typical dry history textbook. It's history with a bit of Ryan Reynolds humor, Jim Halpert's looks to the camera, and Kevin Hart's audaciousness. This is not going to be a series of dates followed by a random dude's name and then another date, and then a war.

Making Sense of This Book

You're probably wondering how to best navigate through this book. This isn't a labyrinth, and there's no Minotaur at the end (that's Greek mythology). Here's a quick rundown on how to make the most of your journey through Rome's rise and fall.

Firstly, while we've structured this book to flow like the Tiber River, from Rome's shining glory to its dramatic downfall, you're not shackled to a linear path. Jump around if you like. If you're itching to learn about those pesky barbarians before exploring the political shenanigans in Rome, go for it!

Secondly, don't rush. This isn't a chariot race. Take your time to soak in the rich history, the scandalous tales, and the lessons we can learn. Rome wasn't built in a day, after all.

Lastly, engage with the material. Question it. Challenge it. Picture yourself as a Roman citizen, or even an emperor, and immerse yourself in the narrative.

In essence, this book is your time machine, your Roman tour guide, and your portal to the past. Use it as you please. Just make sure you enjoy it

— CHAPTER 2 —

ROME'S GREATEST HITS COLLECTION

Rome's Stretch Marks: The Unplanned Growth Spurt

Picture this: you're a bird soaring over the ancient world, a feathery drone, if you will. Beneath you, an empire expands in all directions, like someone gave Romans the cheat codes to unlimited growth in a civilization-building video game. That sprawling spectacle, my friend, is the Roman Empire in its radiant prime.

Now, the Romans didn't do things by halves. When they decided to build an empire, they didn't just take over the neighboring city-states. Oh no, they went for the whole shebang. At its zenith, around 117 AD under Emperor Trajan, the empire stretched from the misty moors of Scotland (then known as Caledonia) to the sun-drenched sands of northern Africa. It extended eastward to the Black Sea, and westward to the Atlantic Ocean. That's around 5 million square kilometers of land - bigger than India!

The Romans weren't just hoarding land for the sake of it. They were strategic, choosing areas rich in resources, strategically located for trade, or both. Picture prime real estate spanning three continents. The empire boasted a smorgasbord of cultures, climates, and terrains - from the vineyards of Gaul (modern-day France) and the silver mines of Hispania (Spain), to the fertile Nile valley in Egypt and the bustling trade routes of Asia Minor.

But what's an empire without its people, right? And the Roman Empire had people in spades. At its height, it was home to about 60 to 70 million souls, making up roughly 20% of the world's population at the time. That's like cramming the entire current population of the U.K. into a time-traveling phone booth and dumping them in ancient Rome.

And these weren't just Romans. The empire was a bubbling melting pot of cultures and ethnicities - Gauls, Britons, Greeks, Egyptians, Jews, and many others. They were all part of the Roman Empire, each adding their unique flavor to the Roman stew.

Despite the vast distances and cultural differences, the empire was surprisingly well connected. Imagine Roman' highways' - the famous Roman roads - crisscrossing the landscape, enabling the movement of goods, armies, and ideas. Sea routes across the Mediterranean (Mare Nostrum, or 'Our Sea,' as the Romans cheekily called it) buzzed with ships carrying everything from Egyptian grain to Spanish silver and Chinese silk.

So, there you have it. The Roman Empire in all its sprawling, diverse glory. And remember, while you're picturing all this, don't forget to marvel at the audacity, the sheer guts it took to build and maintain such an empire. But as we'll see, managing this beast was no walk in the Roman park...

The Roman Political Machine: Governance and Law

So, we've established that the Romans had a colossal, culturally diverse empire. But how on earth did they manage such a massive expanse of land and sea, and a populace as varied as a box of Bertie Bott's Every Flavor Beans? Welcome to Rome's governance - the marvel of administrative organization and legal ingenuity that kept the empire running smoother than a well-oiled chariot.

The first thing to grasp is that Rome's government wasn't a stagnant institution. Like a fine Roman wine, it matured and evolved over time, moving from a monarchy to a republic, and eventually to an empire. Each form had its unique structure and system, adjusting to the growing needs of an expanding realm.

By the time we hit the imperial era, the emperor was the head honcho. The guy with the final say. For our "The Office" fans, Robert California. But don't mistake this for a pure dictatorship. There were still checks and balances in place, with an intricate bureaucracy helping to keep the wheels of governance turning.

This bureaucracy wasn't just about pushing papyrus. It was responsible for a plethora of tasks, from tax collection and administering justice to maintaining public order and overseeing public works. And it did this across the entire empire, through a network of governors, administrators, and local officials. It's like they had their own ancient version of LinkedIn.

Now, let's talk law. The Romans were legal eagles. They created one of the most sophisticated legal systems the ancient world had ever seen -think contracts, property rights, and a complex court system. The principles they established, like "innocent until proven guilty," still form the bedrock of many legal systems today. So next time you watch a courtroom drama, remember to thank the Romans for their contribution to the plot.

But governance wasn't just about ruling and law-making. It was also about inclusivity. The Romans had this crazy idea - at least for the time - that people from all corners of the empire could become Roman citizens, with all the rights and responsibilities that came with it. This wasn't just for the upper crust, either. Over time, even freed slaves could become citizens.

In 212 AD, Emperor Caracalla went one step further and granted citizenship to all free men within the empire's borders. Imagine that - one day, you're a humble Gaulish farmer, and the next, you're a Roman citizen! This was a masterstroke in fostering unity and loyalty among the empire's diverse population.

Rome was a complex, evolving system that managed to keep an empire of millions functioning, and it did so for centuries.

When Romans Played LEGO: Grand Infrastructure and Lofty Arches

When you think of Rome, what springs to mind -gladiators, emperors, lavish feasts, gelato, pizza? Sure, those are all part of the package. But if there's one thing that really makes Rome stand out from the ancient crowd, it's the architecture. And not just architecture in the "let's build a pretty building" sense, but grand, jaw-dropping, marvel-at-the-ingenuity-of-ancient-engineers kind of architecture. While we are over here trying to decorate a simple gingerbread house or carve a decent pumpkin, these people were creating masterpieces.

First, let's look at the public buildings. These were the stages where Rome played out its power, grandeur, and sophistication. Take the Colosseum, for instance. This gargantuan structure wasn't just a venue for gladiatorial contests, mock sea battles, and public spectacles; it was a showcase of Roman architectural and engineering prowess. Able to hold an estimated 50,000 to 80,000 spectators, the Colosseum was the ultimate entertainment hub, an ancient prototype of a multi-purpose sports arena.

Then there were the temples, the palaces, and the bathhouses, each a masterclass in design and functionality. The Pantheon, with its concrete dome and central opening (oculus), still stands as a testament to Roman ingenuity. This 2,000-year-old temple to the gods is the world's largest unreinforced concrete dome, which is kind of like being the world's oldest living teenager - an impressive paradox.

And let's not forget the Roman baths, the ancient world's equivalent of a leisure center. Think less of a quick dip and more of a day-long social event, complete with hot and cold plunges, exercise rooms, libraries, and even eateries. The Baths of Caracalla in Rome could accommodate over 1,500 bathers at once, making it the ideal place to cleanse, socialize, and show off your latest toga.

But Rome's architectural marvels weren't just confined to buildings. The Romans were master road builders, creating a vast network of highways stretching from Britain to the Middle East. These roads - straight, solid, and reliable, something we can't seem to master today - enabled the efficient movement of troops, goods, and information, kind of like the internet of the ancient world.

And the aqueducts! These engineering wonders transported fresh water from distant sources directly into cities and towns. The Pont du Gard in France, part of a 30-mile-long aqueduct system, is a stunning example of Roman engineering. This three-tiered structure, as tall as a 15-story building, carried water across the Gardon River.

But these architectural masterpieces were more than just practical structures or showpieces. They were symbols of Rome's power, prosperity, and cultural superiority. They embodied the essence of Rome itself, and they continue to amaze us with their grandeur and ingenuity.

Yet, as we'll discover in the next section, even these symbols of strength and permanence had their limitations. The very stones that stood for Rome's glory also bore silent witness to its excesses, its struggles, and ultimately, its decline.

When in Rome: A Smorgasbord of Culture

Just like a slow-cooked Italian ragù, Rome's culture was a blend of flavors, each ingredient contributing to a unique, rich, and vibrant whole. From literature and philosophy to art and education, Roman culture was a heady mix that both absorbed and influenced the ancient world.

Let's start with literature. When it came to crafting captivating tales, the Romans were masters of the art. Just as J.K. Rowling has invigorated our modern imaginations, so too did Virgil and Ovid shape the myths and legends of their time. In parallel, Juvenal and Horace, akin to the sharp wit of figures like Charlie Chaplin or Mark Twain, used satire to expose the shortcomings of Roman society. And let's not forget the historians - Livy, Tacitus, Suetonius - who provided us with a precious window into Rome's past. They were the Stephen Kings of their era, masterfully crafting narratives that bring the past to life and make the experience of reading Rome's history as gripping as a suspense thriller. These literary heavyweights didn't just entertain; they helped shape the moral and cultural values of Roman society.

Rome wasn't all about tales of gods and heroes, however. Philosophy also played a vital role in Roman culture. Stoicism, with its emphasis on virtue, duty, and acceptance, was particularly popular, influencing everyone from slaves to emperors. Think of it as ancient Rome's self-help guide, helping Romans navigate the trials and tribulations of life.

Art, too, was a vital part of Roman culture. From grand public sculptures and intricate mosaics to the breathtaking frescoes of Pompeii, Roman art was diverse and dynamic. It wasn't just about aesthetics; art served various purposes, from showcasing Roman might to telling moral tales. It was, in essence, a visual language that spoke volumes about Roman identity and values.

Then there was education. In Rome, education wasn't just for the elite. Children, regardless of their social status, were taught to read and write. Higher education included grammar, rhetoric, philosophy, and even military training. In a way, the Roman education system was a cultural melting pot in miniature, blending elements of literature, philosophy, and physical education to shape the citizens of tomorrow.

As you can see, Rome was more than just an empire. It was a vibrant, diverse cultural hub that absorbed and reimagined influences from the wider ancient world. Its cultural legacy - the stories, ideas, images, and values that it produced - is still with us today, shaping our own understanding of the world.

So, the next time you find yourself chuckling at a satirical cartoon, pondering a philosophical conundrum, or admiring a piece of public art, remember - you're part of a tradition that goes back to the Romans.

Pax Romana:

When Rome Finally Decided to Take a Chill Pill

Oh, to be in Rome during the Pax Romana! Imagine a two-century-long party where the wine never ran out, the music never stopped, and you didn't have to check over your shoulder for a marauding barbarian every five minutes. Well, it wasn't quite like that, but the Pax Romana was indeed a golden age of stability, prosperity, and – dare I say it – peace.

Starting with the reign of Emperor Augustus in 27 B.C., the Pax Romana (Latin for "Roman Peace") stretched all the way to 180 AD. Now, "peace" is a relative term, especially for the Romans. It didn't mean they'd given up their favorite pastime of conquering new territories or that gladiatorial games were replaced with knitting contests. No, it simply meant that the large-scale wars that had marked the Republic era had subsided, and Rome was no longer in constant expansion mode. It was the equivalent of defending your established territory in Risk and just conquering a new country here and there rather than completely obliterating your friend's army in a single turn.

So, what did the Romans do with all this spare time on their hands? They prospered, that's what. With a stable political climate and a booming economy, Rome became the ancient world's equivalent of Wall Street and Silicon Valley rolled into one. Trade flourished, both within the empire and beyond, as Roman goods made their way to distant markets. The Romans were particularly adept at engineering and manufacturing, producing goods ranging from the mundane (pottery, textiles) to the magnificent (statues, jewelry).

In the absence of war, arts and culture flourished. This was the era when Virgil crafted the *Aeneid*, a sweeping epic that tells the story of Aeneas, a Trojan who became an ancestor of the Romans. Meanwhile, Ovid penned his *Metamorphoses*, a collection of mythological and legendary tales with transformation as a central theme. Vitruvius, the architect, was busy constructing revolutionary buildings, setting standards for architecture that remain influential. With tranquility at the borders, Rome was free to focus on cultivating its internal identity - a task it accomplished with a fervor that continues to echo in our world today.

However, it wasn't just about money and culture. The Pax Romana was also a time of social and political stability. Laws were standardized across the empire, a postal system was established, and Rome built an extensive network of roads, which served both military and commercial purposes. And in what could be considered the ancient version of a VIP pass, Roman citizenship was extended beyond Italy, an act that helped integrate the diverse populations of the empire.

However, as we'll see in the next chapter, the Pax Romana wasn't all sunshine and olive oil. Underneath the surface, tensions were brewing - tensions that would eventually lead to cracks in the glorious facade of the Roman Empire. But for now, let's raise a cup of Roman wine to the Pax Romana, an era when Rome truly felt like the eternal city.

Embracing Everyone:
Rome's Multicultural Hug (Some Restrictions Apply)

If the Roman Empire were a modern-day party, it would be the ultimate potluck dinner. Everyone was invited, everyone brought something to the table, and the result was a diverse, vibrant feast of cultures that is still unrivaled today.

Welcome to the spirit of Rome - a spirit of inclusivity and multiculturalism.

The Roman Empire, at its height, stretched from the sun-kissed sands of North Africa to the rain-drenched lands of Britain, encompassing a vast array of cultures, languages, and religions. Now, managing such a diverse crowd would have been as chaotic as teaching salsa dancing to a room full of cats. But the Romans, bless their togas, had a knack for organization and a surprisingly modern attitude towards diversity.

Firstly, Rome was quite the trailblazer in the realm of inclusivity. They weren't just inviting new friends to their weekly book club; they were offering full-blown citizenship to those they conquered. And this wasn't some cut-rate, bottom-tier citizenship either. This was the platinum-level, airport-lounge-access, red-carpet-rolled-out kind of deal, complete with legal protection, voting rights, and even the chance to run for public office. The result? A giant melting pot of cultures united under the Roman banner, embodying the original 'we are the world' spirit.

But it wasn't just about citizenship. The Romans were also champions of cultural integration. They allowed, and often encouraged, the cultures within their empire to retain their customs, languages, and religions. This policy of multiculturalism not only kept the peace but also enriched Roman culture, creating a vibrant tapestry of traditions that is still visible in the remnants of the empire today.

Let's take religion, for example. The Romans were known for their religious tolerance, allowing the worship of various gods and goddesses within the empire. This spiritual smorgasbord ranged from the traditional Roman Pantheon to Eastern cults like Mithraism and, eventually, to Christianity. This religious diversity, while sometimes a source of conflict, was also a testament to Rome's welcoming spirit.

The Roman Empire, the ultimate melting pot, where diversity was not just tolerated but embraced, and where a spirit of inclusivity helped forge one of the most powerful empires in history. Yet, as we'll see in the next chapter, even the most inclusive of empires has its breaking point

CHAPTER 3

ROME'S CHECK
ENGINE LIGHT WAS DEFINITELY ON

Plot Twists and Power Plays

In the good old days of the Pax Romana, being a Roman emperor was a pretty sweet gig. You got to wear a fancy laurel wreath, you could eat whatever you wanted, people literally thought you were a god, and you had an entire empire at your sandaled feet. In essence, they had all the perks of a modern-day house cat. But as time went on, the imperial office started to resemble less a divine appointment and more a game of musical chairs - with daggers.

Welcome to the world of Roman political corruption and power struggles, where backstabbing was literal, and the stakes were as high as the empire itself.

Let's set the scene. Imagine you're at a typical Roman banquet, reclining on plush couches, feasting on stuffed dormice (yes, that's exactly what it sounds like), and flamingo tongues (seriously), with a live band serenading you. Sounds like a perfect evening, doesn't it? But there's a catch - your host is the emperor, and the wine being poured by a dutiful servant could be just as easily laced with poison as it could be a fine vintage. Multiply this level of paranoia and danger by a hundred, and you start to get a sense of the cutthroat political climate in late Rome.

From the outside, Rome seemed invincible. But on the inside, it was a hot mess of political corruption and power struggles. Emperors were frequently overthrown or assassinated by ambitious underlings, rivals, or even their own guards. In fact, during the "Crisis of the Third Century," Rome had a whopping 26 claimants to the throne in just 50 years. Talk about job insecurity!

The Senate, once the powerhouse of the Roman Republic, was now primarily a rubber-stamp institution, its members either too scared or too corrupt to challenge the emperor. And let's not even get started on the rampant bribery, embezzlement, and tax evasion. Essentially, Rome was beginning to look like your favorite political drama series, only with more toga parties and zero technology.

Why does all this political drama matter, you ask? Well, these power struggles and corruption undermined the stability of the empire. They led to inconsistent leadership, frequent civil wars, and a general decline in public trust in the government. In other words, Rome was slowly tearing itself apart from the inside, and the barbarians hadn't even shown up yet!

We're about to dive into the messy, dramatic, and frankly soap opera-esque decline of the Roman Empire. It'll be like watching the ancient world's juiciest reality show: "Keeping Up with the Caesars"!

On the Empire's
Pocketbook and Its Occasional Emptiness

Just when you thought things couldn't get any worse in the Empire (Spoiler Alert: they could, and they did), the economy decided to join the party. And not in a fun, "let's have a couple of drinks and dance and give everyone a ton of stimulus money" kind of way. More like the "I'm going to ruin everything" kind of way. Welcome to the Roman Empire's economic turmoil.

Let's start with inflation. Rome didn't have a central bank to control its money supply or someone to scowl at anyone who suggested creating more coins. So, when the government needed money, they just minted more coins. That sounds like a great idea, right? Well, not exactly. With more coins in circulation, the value of each coin decreased, leading to inflation. Before you knew it, a loaf of bread cost a small fortune, and people were hauling their money in wheelbarrows. Okay, maybe not wheelbarrows, but you get the point.

Then there were the taxes. Oh, the taxes. To fund their lavish lifestyles and constant wars, Roman emperors needed money - lots of it. So, they turned to their favorite cash cow: the people. Taxes skyrocketed, and not in a fun, "let's build more schools and hospitals or an amusement park to boost the morale of the people" kind of way. More like the "I can't afford to eat because of the tax bill" kind of way.

And let's not forget about unemployment. With the influx of enslaved people from conquered territories, many free Roman citizens found themselves out of work. Not to mention the small businesses that couldn't compete with the wealthy elite's vast estates. The result? High unemployment and a lot of very unhappy Romans.

In essence, Rome was in the throes of an economic disaster. Picture it as a leaking boat where every hole causes more water to rush in, each one compounding the problem of the others. The political corruption, the social unrest, the military overspending - all these issues were only heightened and worsened by the relentless waves of the economic crisis.

As we proceed on our journey through the decline of the Roman Empire, keep this in mind - the fall wasn't simply the result of political intrigues or barbarian invasions. The economy, as quiet as it may seem, played a pivotal role as well.

Slouching Morality and
Roman Society's Cringeworthy Moments

On top of political turmoil and economic crisis, Rome had yet another guest to its "Decline and Fall" party: societal issues and public discontent. And no, this wasn't the fun kind of party guest who brought a great dip and made everyone laugh. This was the kind that insulted your décor, spilled red wine on your white couch, and started a fight. Welcome to the Roman moral decay.

Ah, Rome. Home to grand coliseums, beautiful mosaics, and... moral decay? As the empire expanded, so did the gap between the rich and the poor. The wealthy elites lived in luxury, throwing extravagant parties with exotic foods, enjoying hot baths, and generally living it up. Meanwhile, the average Joe (or should I say, the average Julius) was struggling to put food on the table.

This vast wealth inequality was just one facet of Rome's moral decay. Another was the decline in traditional Roman values. Frugality, discipline, and respect for the gods—once the hallmarks of Roman society—were being replaced by extravagance, laziness, and skepticism.

Then there was the public discontent. Imagine being a Roman citizen, watching the rich get richer while your own pocket felt emptier. You'd be pretty miffed, right? Now add in high taxes, rampant corruption, and a lack of job opportunities, and you've got a recipe for some seriously unhappy Romans. Public discontent was high, and faith in the empire was wavering.

It wasn't all doom and gloom, of course. There were still plenty of Romans who believed in their empire, who upheld traditional values, and worked hard for their city, but the cracks were showing. The empire that had once seemed invincible was now looking a little worse for wear. And the moral decay was a symptom of a much larger disease.

So, as we continue our journey through Rome's decline, remember this: Rome didn't just fall because of invasions, or political instability, or economic crisis. It also fell because of a decline in societal values and public trust. That is a lesson we should all take to heart.

Swords, Sandals, and
a Bloated Budget: The Military Quagmire

Now, let's talk about Rome's military budget. Think your country's defense spending is out of control? Oh, sweet summer child, you ain't seen nothing yet. Rome's military budget was like a teenager with a credit card: sky-high and ultimately unsustainable. Welcome to the financial sinkhole that was Rome's defense budget.

Rome had a vast empire to protect, and that didn't come cheap. Soldiers needed to be paid, forts were required to be built, and equipment needed to be replaced. And let's not forget about the wars. Oh, the wars. Rome was constantly fighting off invasions, quelling rebellions, or just plain invading other territories because, well, they could. And all of this came with a hefty price tag.

Rome's solution? More taxes, more coin minting, more debt. This military overspending was like a black hole, sucking in resources from all over the empire. And it wasn't just the money; the human cost was enormous, too. Soldiers were often away for years, leaving their families and farms behind.

But it wasn't just the spending. The legions, once Rome's pride and joy, were also facing problems. Recruitment was down, morale was low, and loyalty... well, let's just say some legions were more loyal to their generals than to Rome. Not exactly what you want in a fighting force.

And so, the military, once the backbone of the Roman Empire, became yet another crack in its foundation. It was bleeding money, losing support, and failing to protect the empire as effectively as it once had. The cost of defense, it turned out, was much higher than anyone had anticipated. So as we delve deeper into Rome's decline, let's remember this: a strong military was essential, but it's wasn't everything. And when the cost of defense became a burden rather than a benefit, well, Rome was on the road to falling.

The Trouble with Having
Too Much Land and Not Enough Fences

Rome, in its heyday, was like that kid in the candy store who just couldn't stop at one. You know the one. They'd take a bit of this, a bit of that, until their pockets were overflowing, and they couldn't quite manage to hold onto everything (I'll be honest... that was me). Rome's insatiable appetite for expansion was impressive...until it wasn't. Welcome to the complications of overexpansion.

When Rome was smaller, management was simple. Imagine running a lemonade stand; it's pretty easy, right? You make the lemonade, serve it to customers, and collect the money. Now imagine running 50 lemonade stands, spread out over thousands of miles, all at once. Suddenly, things aren't so simple. This was Rome, except with provinces instead of lemonade stands, and rebellions instead of thirsty customers.

Each new territory the Romans acquired was essentially a package deal - they didn't just gain land, but also an assortment of distinct cultures, languages, religions, and customs, each with their own unique challenges. Each new province needed a governor, an army, roads, and infrastructure. Cultural diversity was a strength of the empire, but also a challenge. Not everyone was thrilled about becoming Roman, and rebellions were common.

Then there was the military strain. Soldiers were spread thin across the empire, defending borders from Britain to the Middle East. Communication was slow, making it challenging to respond swiftly to threats. And the more they expanded, the more enemies they made. Rome was like the popular kid at school who made a few too many enemies.

In the end, the cost of expansion simply outweighed the benefits. The Romans were great at conquering, but managing an empire of that size? That was another story. It was like trying to juggle while riding a unicycle, blindfolded. And Rome, it seems, was about to drop the ball.

Bigger isn't always better. And as Rome learned the hard way, overextending your boundaries can have some severe consequences

— CHAPTER 4 —

BARBARIANS AT THE
GATE (AND EVERYWHERE ELSE)

When Unruly
Neighbors Came Knocking... with Axes

So, we have examined Rome, the superpower of the ancient world - the place where togas were in vogue and gladiatorial games were the weekend highlight. Now, let's shift our attention to the barbarians. No, we're not delving into the realm of fantasy novels where these figures are portrayed with rippling muscles, improbable combat skills, and questionable fashion choices. We're referring to the flesh-and-blood people who resided on the fringes of the Roman Empire, the ones who brought about a dramatic climax to Rome's hitherto unshakeable narrative. It's time to peek behind the Roman marble and into the tumultuous world of Gothic sieges, Vandal raids, and Hunnic invasions - welcome to the less glamorous side of antiquity.

The term "barbarian" was Rome's courteous way of labeling anyone who didn't speak Latin or Greek and who lived beyond the comfort of their empire. They were deemed uncivilized, but this title was somewhat misleading. Beneath the perceived uncouth exterior, these so-called barbarians were in fact part of complex societies rich with unique cultures and traditions.

Let's start with the Goths. This group of disgruntled Germanic tribes didn't particularly appreciate being under the Roman thumb, and who can blame them? After a series of dubious agreements and mistreatments, the Goths decided they'd had enough and revolted. The Battle of Adrianople in 378 A.D. was kind of like Rome stepping on a LEGO brick in the middle of the night - unexpected, intensely painful, and deeply rattling. In this historic conflict, the Goths didn't merely defeat the Romans, they steamrolled over them. They killed the Eastern Roman Emperor Valens and left the Roman army in a state of shock, their sense of invincibility significantly dented.

Next, we're off to 410 A.D., when the Visigoths, led by Alaric, gave Rome a makeover nobody asked for. Yes, the Eternal City had faced destruction before, but this... this was a whole new level. For the first time in 800 years, Rome crumbled under the power of a foreign enemy. The psychological fallout was immense. It was like tuning into the Oscars and watching Will Smith slap Chris Rock across the face – jaw-dropping, disheartening, and a glaring signal that the proverbial wheels were coming off.

Then we have the Vandals, a group so adept at destructive exploits that their name has become eternally associated with mindless destruction. If you ever wondered where the term "vandalism" came from, well, now you know. Their raids were notorious, but their sacking of Rome in 455 A.D. became their crowning glory. This time, it was less of a shock and more of a confirmation that Rome was in serious trouble. The city was plundered for two weeks, and the event marked a further step in Rome's decline.

Next, the Huns, led by the infamous Attila, were known for their fierce warrior culture and nomadic lifestyle. These were the folks who came for dinner uninvited and then refused to leave. They might not have directly invaded Rome, but their incessant pressure on the other barbarian tribes created a chain reaction, pushing tribes like the Goths right into Roman territory. Their influence on the trajectory of Rome's history, therefore, is indisputable.

Each of these invasions chipped away at the already fraying edges of the Roman Empire. The military was stretched thin, the economy was strained, and the people were tired. The barbarian invasions were like that annoying younger sibling who keeps poking you during a long car ride. Eventually, you just can't take it anymore.

To cap it all, there's the final curtain call in 476 A.D., the fall of the Western Roman Empire when Odoacer, a Germanic chieftain, deposed Romulus Augustulus. Though not a climactic battle per se, it marked the official end of the line for the Western Roman Empire.

So, the next time you hear the term "barbarian," remember they were far more than Rome's occasional annoyance. They were the catalyst that sent Rome spiraling down the staircase of decline. These invasions and battles were not just military failures; they were an early indication of a world undergoing massive change, a change that didn't stop with the fall of Rome but continued to shape history long after.

Rome's Reaction:
Trying to Shoo Away Pesky Invaders

Imagine you're in a boat. It's a nice boat, well built. But then you notice a tiny leak. You plug it with some chewing gum, no problem. But then there's another leak... and another... and another. Suddenly, your boat resembles a block of Swiss cheese. That's the situation Rome found itself in with these barbarian invasions. Let's look at how Rome, with its sinking ship, tried to keep afloat amidst this chaos.

Initially, Rome tried to integrate the barbarian tribes, like the Goths, into the Empire. A clever plan, right? "Join us, and let's be friends," they said. The Goths were granted lands and were even allowed to join the Roman military. But the Romans treated them poorly, leading to resentment, rebellion, and ultimately, the Battle of Adrianople. So, that plan backfired.

Next, they attempted diplomatic negotiations. For instance, when Attila the Hun came knocking, Emperor Valentinian III sent Pope Leo I to negotiate peace. Surprisingly, it worked. Attila withdrew, and Rome breathed a sigh of relief. But relying on negotiations was like using a band-aid for a bullet wound. It did little to address the underlying issues.

Then there were the military reforms. Emperors like Diocletian and Constantine reorganized the army, built fortifications, and even split the Empire in two to make it more manageable. But these were short-term fixes. Over time, the Empire became too dependent on barbarian soldiers, who were not always loyal to Rome.

Finally, in desperation, some emperors even tried paying off the barbarians, offering them money or land to stop their attacks. This was the equivalent of giving a cookie to a naughty child, hoping they'll behave. It worked about as well as you might expect.

In the end, Rome's responses were like sticking fingers in a leaking dam. Each solution seemed like a good idea at the time but ultimately failed to address the fundamental problems. The invasions continued, the Empire weakened, and the once-mighty Rome could no longer hold back the tide of change.

The Cumulative Weight of Unwanted Visitors

Now that we've seen the Romans scrambling around, trying to deal with these invasions, let's talk about the fallout. If Rome was a grand old mansion, the attacks were like termites, slowly but surely eating away at its foundations.

Firstly, let's talk money. Maintaining an army to counter these invasions was expensive. Rome was bleeding money, and the economy was suffering. Imagine throwing a lavish party when you can't pay the electricity bill – not the best idea, right? Taxes increased, and inflation soared. The once vibrant markets began to look more like a yard sale at the end of the day.

Secondly, the invasions disrupted trade. Remember learning about the Silk Road in school? Not the dark web version, but the ancient trade route? It was like Rome's Amazon Prime, delivering goods from across the empire. But now, with barbarians running amok, trade routes were often blocked, leading to shortages and a further blow to the economy.

Thirdly, there was the societal impact. As cities were sacked and territories lost, the once-proud Romans lived in constant fear and uncertainty. It's hard to focus on your vineyard when you're worried about a Goth hiding in the bushes.

Then there was the psychological effect. Remember when the Visigoths sacked Rome in 410 A.D.? That was a massive blow to Roman pride. It's like when you trip and fall in public. You might not be physically hurt, but oh boy, your ego takes a beating.

Lastly, the invasions led to a shift in power. As the Western Roman Empire crumbled under the weight of the raids, the Eastern Roman Empire, later known as the Byzantine Empire, began to rise in prominence. But that's a story for another day.

In essence, the invasions were like the world's worst house guests, overstaying their welcome, trashing the place, and leaving Rome with a hefty clean-up bill. They accelerated Rome's decline, making the fall of the Empire not a question of if, but when

CHAPTER 5

CHRISTIANITY ENTERS THE CHAT

Christianity: The Plot Twist No One Saw Coming

P icture this: you're a Roman citizen, accustomed to a smorgasbord of gods and goddesses, each with their own domain and quirks, and then along comes a religion preaching just one God. Sounds radical, doesn't it? Well, welcome to the rise of Christianity in Rome.

Christianity entered the Roman Empire's stage in the 1st century A.D., not with a bang but as a subtle murmur, comparable to an obscure piece of music slowly gaining recognition. The early followers of this burgeoning religion were often in peril and at risk of intense persecution. Nero, the infamous emperor, did not hesitate to blame them for the Great Fire of Rome in 64 A.D., causing their plight to be more dire. Quite the precarious start for a faith that would eventually reshape the empire and the world.

Despite these hardships, Christianity began to gain traction, primarily due to its appeal to the underprivileged. After all, it offered hope, salvation, and a sense of community, which was quite the package deal in a society now rife with inequality.

But the real game-changer was Emperor Constantine's conversion to Christianity in the 4th century. Think of it as getting a celebrity endorsement. Constantine didn't just like Christianity; he put it on the empire's "Top Hits" by issuing the Edict of Milan in 313 AD, which granted religious freedom to all. Overnight, Christianity went from being the underdog to the official religion of the Empire.

But it wasn't all smooth sailing. The shift from a multi-god society to a single-god society was a significant upheaval. The Romans went from a plethora of gods to following one – it was a substantial shift in religious, societal, and cultural norms. But why, and how did this change Rome?

When Romans
Swapped Wine Gods for Wine and Communion

First off, it's important to note that Romans were no strangers to religion. They had gods for everything - love, war, wine, you name it. Religion was a part of everyday life. But with Christianity, there was a significant shift. Instead of many gods,

there was now just one. Instead of sacrifices and festivals to the Roman gods, there were prayers and sermons to a single God.

Christianity brought a new moral code to society. It emphasized virtues like humility, charity, and forgiveness - quite a change from the "might makes right" mentality of the Romans. "Love thy neighbor," said Christ, even if thy neighbor is a Goth who just raided your vineyard.

The Church also began to play a significant role in society. It became a source of education, charity, and social services. Picture it as a kind of ancient non-profit organization, providing support to those in need.

Furthermore, Christianity also changed the power dynamics in Rome. The Church became a new power center, often clashing with the traditional Roman authority who still looked to the old gods. Emperors like Constantine eventually used Christianity to unify the Empire, sort of like a spiritual glue.

However, this transition wasn't smooth. There was conflict, persecution, and resistance. Imagine convincing a society used to worshiping a pantheon of gods to switch to just one. For the ancient Romans, it would have been like convincing a kid to trade a bag of candy for a single piece, no matter how mighty and big that piece was.

From Gladiators to Gospel: A Divine Rebranding

So, Rome has gone from a divine buffet of gods to just one in Christianity. How did this new faith shake up society? Well, it was like dropping Mentos into a bottle of Diet Coke. Let's break down the fizz.

Let's start with the biggies - slavery and gladiatorial games. Christianity didn't exactly abolish these practices, but it did begin to change attitudes toward them. Slaves were seen as equal in the eyes of God, and while that didn't translate to instant freedom, it did give enslaved people a sense of dignity and hope. As for gladiatorial games, well, Christians weren't too keen on the whole "killing for entertainment" thing. Over time, these games became less popular and were eventually phased out.

Then there were the changes in societal structure. The Church became a sort of social safety net, providing aid to the poor, caring for the sick, and generally stepping in where the Roman state failed. It was like the world's first welfare system, minus the paperwork.

The concept of charity, a cornerstone of Christian teaching, also began to permeate society. Giving to the poor, helping the needy, sharing your wealth – these ideas were revolutionary at the time, and they started to change the way Romans thought about wealth and poverty.

Finally, Christianity shifted the balance of power in society. The Church became a new power center, sometimes clashing with traditional Roman authority. This shift played a massive role in the later stages of the Empire and had a profound impact on the course of Western history, not least by providing a moral compass and unifying force during times of deep fragmentation and societal upheaval.

In essence, Christianity provided Roman society with a spiritual facelift, shifting attitudes, actions, and hierarchies. This was not a mere evolution but a religious revolution, echoing down the centuries to this day. So the next time you consider acts of kindness, remember it's part of a legacy left by the Christian Romans - they laid the foundation for the ethos of charity we recognize today.

When Soldiers Pondered Turning the Other Cheek

You've probably already guessed that the change was tough for the Roman military. One minute they're the cream of the crop, the next, they're dealing with pacifism. It's like trying to defend against sharks with goldfish. So, how did the Christian faith impact Rome's military might?

Firstly, let's get this straight: Christianity and the military were about as comfortable together as a cat and a vacuum cleaner. The Christian faith preached love, forgiveness, and turning the other cheek, while the Roman military was all about discipline, fighting, and, well, not turning the other cheek. The New Testament wasn't exactly a handbook for warfare. Jesus' teachings leaned heavily towards peace, advocating non-violence and love for one's enemies - not exactly the sort of thing you want to hear when you're trying to rally the troops.

It wasn't like the entire Roman military suddenly replaced their sharpened swords with the Scripture. The path to Christianity resembled more of a marathon than a sprint, with many soldiers and generals continuing to hold tightly onto their tried-and-true beliefs. Yet, as Christianity began to thread its influence through the fabric of Roman society, it created a nuanced tug-of-war, not unlike when a staunch traditionalist finds himself sharing the dinner table with a radical innovator - a bit of tension, a dash of intrigue, and a whole lot of change in the air.

Some Christian soldiers grappled with the contradiction of their faith and their duty. There were even instances of soldiers refusing to fight, or deserting the army, citing their Christian beliefs. This wasn't exactly ideal for Rome's defense strategy. It's tough to maintain a fearsome reputation when some of your soldiers are more interested in caring for others than killing others.

Then there was the issue of rituals. The Roman army was steeped in pagan traditions – sacrifices before battles, prayers to Mars, the god of war, that sort of thing. With the spread of

Christianity, these rituals began to fade away, leading to a sort of identity crisis within the ranks.

All of this isn't to say that Christianity was the sole actor in the theater of Rome's military decline. Like any complex historical event, there were many moving parts - economic turbulence, the stresses of overexpansion, and more. Yet Christianity introduced a transformative ethos into the mix. With a growing emphasis on peace and love for one's neighbor, it added a new dimension to the narrative of the Roman Empire, subtly reshaping its approach to power and conflict by shifting the Empire's values and priorities.

In short, the Roman military and Christianity were a bit like oil and water – they just didn't mix. And while Rome tried its best to shake things up, in the end, the mixture just wouldn't blend.

— CHAPTER 6 —

THE EMPIRE SPLITS:
IT'S NOT ME, IT'S YOU

East or West: Rome's Biggest Game of Eenie Meenie

Like two siblings growing up in the same home but destined for starkly different lives, the Eastern and Western Roman Empires, though born of the same stock, would follow paths as different as the setting sun and the rising moon. Splitting the empire was like turning a chart-topping rock band into two solo acts. Think of it as if John Lennon and Paul McCartney each started their own Beatles while still playing the old hits. You could enjoy the tunes, but you wouldn't be able to help feeling that something was missing.

The Western Empire was the more "popular" sibling, so to speak. Rome, with its hustle and bustle, its amphitheaters, and palaces, was the beating heart of the West. And yet, as everyone will all too painfully learn, popularity in high school - or in the high-stakes game of ancient empire management - does not always last.

The Eastern Empire, headquartered in Byzantium or as it was later known, Constantinople, took a more low-key approach. While the West was putting on a brave face, internally hemorrhaging from corruption, economic crises, and outside invasions, the East was quietly and methodically shoring up its defenses, keeping its coffers full, and generally not throwing its resources down the Colosseum toilet.

One might ask, "Why the difference?" After all, didn't they share the same DNA? The same glorious Roman heritage? A delightful question, but akin to asking why one twin becomes a virtuoso violinist, and the other can't carry a tune in a bucket, which is by far the easiest container to carry a tune in. Circumstances, my friend, circumstances.

The Eastern Empire was fortunate in geography, blessed by trade routes and far enough away from the pesky barbarian hordes that seemed to have the Western Empire on speed dial. It also enjoyed relative stability in leadership, not having to replace its CEOs every few years in a blaze of backstabbing and general unpleasantness.

Does this mean the East was without fault? Oh, far from it. There was still plenty of regular office politics, scandals, and the occasional violent coup. But compared to the West, it was a model of best practices, a case study in "how to run an empire without it collapsing in a heap of ashes and broken dreams."

What lessons, then, can we pluck from this poignant tale of two empires? Could the Western Empire have avoided its inglorious end by taking a page from its Eastern sibling's playbook? Hindsight, as they say, is 20/20. But it's also as useful as a chocolate teapot when your empire is in ashes.

In essence, while we are of the same origins, our fates may diverge depending on the paths we take, the choices we make, and sometimes, just the plain roll of the dice. The Eastern Empire would continue, reborn as the Byzantine Empire, but that, as they say, is another story for another book.

Emperors' Swansong:
Rome's Last Hurrahs and Whoopsies

Well, folks, we've hit the twilight years of Rome, where the emperors were more like fading stars than blazing suns. It was like watching a TV show where the characters start off strong, but by the end, they're just shadows of their former selves. Let's take a look at the final lineup of Rome's "Who's Who."

First up, we have Honorius, reigning from 395 to 423 AD. A teenager when he ascended to the throne, Honorius had the misfortune of being at the helm during the Visigothic sack of Rome in 410 AD. Despite his lack of effective leadership, he somehow managed to stick around for almost three decades. Think of him as the guy who somehow keeps his job despite lying on his resume and being perpetually confused.

Next, we have Valentinian III, who took over the Western throne in 425 AD and managed to stay there until 455 AD. Valentinian is perhaps best remembered for his scandalous personal life and his inability to prevent the Vandals from sacking Rome in 455 AD. It's no surprise that he was assassinated.

Then there's Majorian, who took the throne in 457 AD and had the chutzpah to actually try and restore the Roman Empire. Despite his best efforts, he was unable to prevent the continued decline and was eventually betrayed and killed by his own general, Ricimer.

Lastly, we have the aptly named Romulus Augustus, the last of the Roman emperors, who ruled for just a single year before being deposed by the Germanic King Odoacer in 476 AD. As the last Roman emperor, Romulus Augustus was more of a whimper than a bang. His reign marked the official end of the Western Roman Empire, bringing the curtain down on a drama that had lasted for over a thousand years.

In the end, the Roman empire near its end had a lineup of emperors who, despite their best (or worst) efforts, couldn't stop the sands of time from running out. They were the captains of a sinking ship, the last leaders of an empire that was once the most powerful in the world. It's a bit like watching a Shakespearean tragedy, isn't it? As Shakespeare says, "All the world's a stage."

Rome's No-so-Golden Retirement Years

We've looked at the build-up and long-standing issues that eventually led to the fall of Rome. Let's now take a look at the state of the Empire at its end. The twilight years were not exactly pretty. Imagine a once-majestic lion, now old and weak, struggling to maintain control of its territory. This was Rome, and it wasn't pretty.

Political conditions: The political situation was about as stable as a three-legged chair. The central government was weak, corruption was rampant, and power was often seized by the military. This resulted in the revolving door of emperors, with more than 20 taking the throne in just 75 years.

Social conditions: If the political situation was a three-legged chair, the social situation was a two-legged stool. The divide between the rich and the poor was vast, and social mobility was almost nonexistent. The wealthy lived in luxury while the masses struggled with poverty, high taxes, and unemployment. It's like the 1% and the 99%, Roman style.

Economic conditions: Economically, Rome was in a state of freefall. Inflation was sky-high, the currency was devalued, and trade was disrupted by constant wars. The government resorted to raising taxes, which only further burdened the poor. It was like trying to put out a fire with gasoline.

Military conditions: The military, once the pride of Rome, was stretched thin and struggling. They were spread out across the empire, defending against constant threats from barbarian invasions. Morale was low, and loyalty was often to the highest bidder rather than to Rome itself.

Religious conditions: The rise of Christianity brought about a significant shift in Roman society. The traditional Roman gods were gradually replaced by the monotheistic Christian faith. This change created tension and conflict, further destabilizing the empire.

So, there you have it. The state of the empire in the end was a cocktail of political instability, social inequality, economic decline, military overstretch, and religious change. It's enough to make anyone pull their hair out. But remember folks, Rome wasn't all doom and gloom. It was also a place of outstanding achievements, innovations, and cultural milestones. So, let's raise our glasses to Rome, for better or for worse

— CHAPTER 7 —

PICKING UP THE ROMAN PIECES

The Morning After the Empire:
Who's Cleaning This Up?

With Rome in ruins, we're now tasked with sifting through the smoldering embers of history. If you thought Rome's decline was akin to a compelling drama, the aftermath isn't simply an encore, it's an entirely new act penned in the ink of resilience and resurgence.

First off, let's talk about the chaos. With no central government, the Western Roman Empire was like a ship without a captain. Different regions tried to fill the power vacuum, leading to a lot of squabbling and infighting. It's like when the teacher leaves the classroom, and everyone starts arguing about who's in charge.

Fiscal shockwaves ricocheted through the once sturdy structures of Rome's economic life. Maritime trade was blown off course, cities were left desolate like stage sets after the curtain falls, and the vibrant pulse of commerce that once coursed through the empire was replaced by a hollow echo. Picture the Dow Jones taking a nosedive, but swap Wall Street for the Roman Forum, and trading screens for wax tablets and styluses.

Culturally, things were equally messy. The fall of Rome led to a loss of knowledge and skills, especially in areas like engineering and literacy. Libraries were destroyed, and much of the knowledge of the Roman world was lost. It's like accidentally deleting your hard drive without a backup.

Of course, one of the most significant changes was the shift in power. With Rome out of the picture, new kingdoms started to emerge, each trying to carve out their own piece of the pie. This period, known as the Migration Period, saw the movement and settlement of Germanic tribes throughout Europe.

From Togas to Chainmail: Europe Goes Medieval

Alright, so Rome has fallen, and we're left with one heck of a mess. But as they say, when one door closes, another opens. So, welcome to the Middle Ages, or as I like to call it, "Rome's awkward teenage years."

The period immediately following the fall of Rome is often referred to as the "Dark Ages," but that's a bit of a misnomer. Sure, there was a decline in learning and culture, and yes, bathing did become a lost art, but it wasn't all doom and gloom. In fact, this period set the stage for some pretty exciting developments down the line.

First off, we see the rise of feudalism. With the Roman government out of the picture, the system of land ownership and allegiance became the new norm. Think of it as a pyramid scheme, but with knights and serfs instead of essential oils. Each layer in the pyramid propped up the layer above it.

With the rise in Christianity, bishops and abbots stepped in to fill the power vacuum, providing stability and order amidst the chaos. It's kind of like when your parents leave town, and your older sibling suddenly becomes the boss.

And let's not forget about the barbarian kingdoms. These guys, once the 'bad boys' of the Roman world, started establishing their own kingdoms, many of which would eventually become modern-day European nations. The Visigoths in Spain, the Ostrogoths and Lombards in Italy, the Franks in France – it was a veritable 'who's who' of the medieval world.

One of the most significant transformations, though, was the shift from a cash economy to a barter system. With the Roman currency devalued, people started trading goods and services instead. It's like swapping your lunch in the school cafeteria, but on a much larger scale.

Enter the Roman-Medieval switcheroo. It might have been a bit rough around the edges, but hey, Rome wasn't built in a day, and it certainly didn't fall in one, either. Now, let's see how this fallen empire shaped the future.

Rome's Hand-Me-Downs: Gifts to Future Generations

Now, let's talk about legacy. You know, like when your grandma leaves you her collection of porcelain cats. Only in this case, the grandma is Rome, and the porcelain cats are... well, let's just get into it.

The legacy of Rome is like a bag of trail mix – there's a bit of everything in there. From law to architecture, from language to government, the fingerprints of Rome can be found all over the modern world.

Take, for instance, the legal system. A lot of our concepts of law and justice come straight from Rome. The idea of "innocent until proven guilty"? Yep, that's a Roman original. The idea of legal representation? Thank the Romans. The practice of writing laws down so everyone could see them? You guessed it – Rome. So, next time you're miffed about that parking fine, just remember it was our Roman forebears who granted us the right to argue about it in the first place.

And then there's the infrastructure. Roads, aqueducts, sewers – the Romans were master builders. Ever heard of a little thing called the Colosseum? That's Roman engineering for you. They even perfected concrete, which is why their buildings are still standing, while ours seem to crumble if you look at them the wrong way.

Let's not forget the language. Latin, the language of Rome, is the ancestor of the Romance languages - that's Italian, French, Spanish, Portuguese, and Romanian for the linguists in the room. And English? Well, we may not be a Romance language, but we've definitely stolen our fair share of Latin terms. For instance, every time you watch a "video" (which means "I see" in Latin), exude "confidence" (deriving from the Latin for "with faith"), or keep a "memento" (Latin for "remember"), you're dipping your toes into Rome's linguistic legacy.

And, of course, there's the concept of the republic. While Rome eventually became an empire, it started as a republic, a form of government where citizens have a say in who governs them. The founding fathers of the United States were huge fans of the Roman Republic and borrowed heavily from it when they drafted the Constitution.

So, Rome might have fallen, but its legacy is alive and well. It's in our laws, our buildings, our language, and our government. It's like Rome never really left. It just put on a pair of sunglasses, changed its name, and blended into the crowd. And that, folks, is the power of legacy.

— CHAPTER 8 —

THE OBLIGATORY
"WE'VE REACHED THE END" BIT

Rome in Review: Just What Was that All About?

S o, here we are, our Roman sojourn drawing to its end. We've shuffled through the ruins, dusted off some historical artifacts, and perhaps shaken our heads in disbelief. All in the noble pursuit of understanding Rome's fall, a task more daunting than trying to finish an extra-large pizza alone. So, let's attempt to make sense of this monumental mess, shall we?

In the course of this book, we journeyed from Rome's glory days, where it was the envy of the ancient world, through to its slow decline and eventual fall. We've watched as Rome, this once-mighty empire, became a victim of its own success, grappling with political corruption, economic turmoil, societal decay, and military overspending.

We've also seen how external threats, particularly the Barbarian invasions, played a crucial role in Rome's downfall. Remember the Visigoths sacking Rome in 410 AD? Or the Vandals doing the same in 455 AD? It's like Rome just couldn't catch a break.

And then there's Christianity. From a persecuted sect to the state religion, we've witnessed how this faith transformed Rome, influencing its society, culture, and even its military.

We've also touched on the transition from Roman to Medieval and seen how, even in its death, Rome managed to shape the future. Rome essentially? passed the baton to the Middle Ages and said, "Here, take this. Don't screw it up."

Keep in mind that history is not just about the rise and fall of empires. It's about understanding the human story, learning from the past, and hopefully, using that knowledge to build a better future.

The Empire's Postmortem: Hindsight's 20/20

Well, we could wrap up our Roman expedition right here, like leaving a movie theater when the credits roll. But that would be as satisfying as ordering a chocolate chip cookie and asking them to hold the chocolate chips - the essence would be missing. Beyond Rome's gripping tale of rise and fall lie lessons, subtle and profound, that have a peculiar habit of echoing through the corridors of history. Let's take a look at some of them.

Lesson 1: The dangers of complacency. Rome didn't fall in a day. It took centuries of neglect, corruption, and internal decay. Rome became complacent in its success, thinking it was invincible. But no empire, no matter how powerful, is immune to decline. The takeaway? Never rest on your laurels. Always strive for better.

Lesson 2: The importance of sustainable growth. Rome expanded too quickly, stretching its resources and creating logistical nightmares. It's like trying to eat a whole pizza in one bite – it's just not going to end well. So, whether you're running an empire, or a lemonade stand, remember: slow and steady wins the race.

Lesson 3: Unity in diversity. Rome was a melting pot of different cultures, and this diversity was one of its strengths. But as the empire declined, this unity fractured, and Rome lost its identity. The lesson here? Diversity is a strength, but only if there's unity and mutual respect.

Lesson 4: The role of values. The rise of Christianity in Rome challenged its traditional values and caused a societal shift. It shows how values can have a major impact on a society's direction.

Lesson 5: The power of resilience. Despite its fall, Rome's legacy lives on in our laws, languages, and governments. It shows that even in decline and death, there can be an enduring influence. So, whatever challenges you face, remember it's not about how you fall. It's about how you get back up and what you leave behind.

Lingered Legacy:
Why We Can't Shut Up About Rome

Why does Rome, an empire that fell over 1,500 years ago, still matter today? Great question. It's not like we're all walking around in togas, right? But despite the time gap, Rome still has a lot to teach us.

So, if you've somehow skipped the rest of the book and landed here, I'll surmise the impact they have on the world today.

Firstly, Rome is everywhere in our modern world. You like democratic republics? Thank Rome for that. The concept of "innocent until proven guilty"? You can thank Rome for that, too. Those Latin phrases you find in law, medicine, and science? Yep, Rome again. It's like Rome is that one person from high school who just keeps popping up in your life.

Secondly, Rome's fall serves as a stark reminder of the dangers of social inequality, political corruption, and economic instability. Sound familiar? It should. These are issues we still grapple with today. Rome's fall teaches us that no society, no matter how advanced, is immune to these problems. It's like a ghost from the past, warning us of the potential pitfalls ahead.

Thirdly, Rome teaches us about the power of cultural integration and the dangers of cultural disintegration. Rome was a melting pot of cultures, and this diversity was a source of its strength. But when this unity broke down, so did Rome. It's a lesson in the importance of maintaining social cohesion in the face of diversity.

Lastly, Rome's transition from polytheism to Christianity provides insight into how religions can shape societies and their values. It's a lesson that's still relevant today, in our increasingly pluralistic and secular societies.

In short, Rome matters because it's a mirror, reflecting our own societies and challenges. And if we can learn from Rome's successes and failures, we can hopefully make our own world a better place.

Goodnight Rome, You Fascinating Mess

So, we've navigated the choppy seas of Rome's grand saga, sailed past emperors decked in power and vanity, confronted barbarians at the doorstep, and witnessed a fresh religious wave washing over the Empire. We've laughed, we've cried, we've pondered deep philosophical questions about the nature of society. Okay, maybe we didn't cry.

As we close this little jaunt through history, let's remember that Rome isn't just a story of the past. It's a lesson for the present and a guide for the future. It's a reminder of the greatness we can achieve, but also the dangers of complacency, corruption, and overreach. It's a testament to the power of diversity, but also the importance of unity.

Above all, Rome is a story of resilience. Despite its fall, its legacy endures, shaping the world we live in today. It's a reminder that even in the face of decline, we can leave a lasting impact. And that, my friend, is a lesson worth remembering.

So here we are, at the end of our journey. It's time to say goodbye to Rome, at least for now. But remember, history isn't just about the past. It's about understanding our present and shaping our future. So keep exploring, keep learning, and who knows? Maybe one day, you'll be the one writing the history books.

Until then, vale! (That's "goodbye" in Latin.)

THE END

APPENDIX

ALL THE WORDS YOU DIDN'T KNOW

Aurelian Walls: Defensive walls around Rome, named after Emperor Aurelian, who initiated their construction.

Barbarians: Term used by Romans to describe tribes from outside the Roman Empire, typically Germanic and Hunnic tribes.

Battle of Adrianople: A key battle in 378 AD where the Eastern Roman Army was defeated by the Visigoths.

Bread and Circuses: A policy of appeasing the masses with food and entertainment.

Byzantium: Eastern continuation of the Roman Empire after the fall of the Western Roman Empire.

Cassiodorus: An important writer, statesman, and monk in the Ostrogothic Kingdom.

Christianity: Religion based on the life and teachings of Jesus Christ, which rose to prominence during the later Roman Empire.

Citizen: A status in Roman society conferring certain rights and responsibilities.

Colosseum: A grand amphitheater in Rome, a symbol of the Roman Empire's might and grandeur.

Constantinople: The capital city of the Roman/Byzantine Empire, and later of the Ottoman Empire, now known as Istanbul.

Consul: One of the highest elected political offices in the Roman Republic.

Decadence: Moral or cultural decline characterized by excessive indulgence in pleasure or luxury.

Diocletian: Roman Emperor from 284 to 305, known for his administrative and military reforms.

Economic inflation: Devaluation of currency and increase in prices.

Emperor: The ruler of the Roman Empire.

Fall of the Roman Empire: The loss of central political control in the Western Roman Empire, a process in which the Empire failed to enforce its rule.

Feudalism: The socio-economic system that followed the fall of the Western Roman Empire.

Fresco: A method of mural painting where pigments are applied to wet plaster, becoming an integral part of the wall as it dries. Known for its durability and vibrant colors, it was commonly used during the Roman period and the Renaissance.

Germanic Tribes: Groups such as the Visigoths, Vandals, and Ostrogoths who invaded the Roman Empire.

Goths: An East Germanic group of tribes who played a key role in the fall of the Roman Empire.

Huns: A nomadic people who invaded Europe and hastened the fall of the Roman Empire.

Invasion: Military incursion into a territory.

Julius Caesar: Prominent Roman general and statesman, played a critical role in the events leading to the demise of the Roman Republic and the rise of the Roman Empire.

Justinian I: Byzantine emperor who attempted to restore the greatness of the Roman Empire.

Latifundia: Large estate system in ancient Rome, the over-reliance on which is often cited as a reason for the fall of Rome.

Legion: The main organizational unit of the Roman Army.

Migration period: The period during which there were widespread migrations of peoples within or into Europe, contributing to the fall of the Roman Empire.

Odoacer: Germanic king who deposed the last Roman emperor, Romulus Augustulus, in 476 AD.

Ostrogoths: A branch of the Goths who played a role in the fall of the Western Roman Empire.

Pagan: A term used to describe religions outside of Christianity, Judaism, and Islam, particularly those practiced in Rome before the adoption of Christianity.

Pax Romana: A period of relative peace and stability across the Roman Empire, which lasted from 27 BC to 180 AD.

Plague of Justinian: A pandemic that afflicted the Byzantine Empire and is thought to have expedited its decline.

Political corruption: The misuse of power by government officials for illegitimate personal gain.

Provinces: Territories outside Italy that were controlled by the Romans.

Republic: The period of ancient Roman civilization where Rome was governed by a system of elected officials.

Roman Senate: Political institution in both the Roman Republic and the Roman Empire.

Romulus Augustulus: Traditionally considered the last emperor of the Western Roman Empire.

Sack of Rome: The three occasions (410, 455, and 476 AD) when the city of Rome was attacked and pillaged.

Senate: The advisory council that helped to govern the ancient city of Rome.

Slavery: The system in which individuals, known as slaves, are treated as property and forced to work.

Tetrarchy: A form of government instituted by Diocletian where the empire was quartered and ruled by four individuals.

Theodosius I: Last emperor to rule over both the eastern and the western halves of the Roman Empire.

Tribute: A payment made periodically by one state or ruler to another as a sign of dependence or submission.

Vandals: East Germanic tribe or group of tribes, famous for sacking Rome in 455 AD.

Vassal State: A state that is subordinate to another.

Visigoths: Branch of the Goths who sacked Rome in 410 AD and later established a kingdom in what is now Spain and Portugal.

Western Roman Empire: The western provinces of the Roman Empire, which fell in 476 AD.

Zeno: Eastern Roman Emperor who negotiated with the Ostrogoths to help protect his territory from other barbarian invasions.

WHEN DID ALL OF THIS HAPPEN?

44 BC: Julius Caesar, the dictator for life, is assassinated by a group of Roman senators.

42 BC: The Liberators' civil war ends with a victory for Mark Antony and Octavian (Julius Caesar's adoptive son) against the forces of Julius Caesar's assassins.

31 BC: Battle of Actium. Octavian's forces defeat the combined forces of Mark Antony and Cleopatra.

27 BC: Octavian is granted the title "Augustus" by the Roman Senate, marking the beginning of the Roman Empire.

AD 14: Death of Augustus, succeeded by his adopted son Tiberius. The Julio-Claudian dynasty continues with the reigns of Caligula, Claudius, and Nero.

30-33 AD: Estimated period of Jesus Christ's crucifixion under the rule of Pontius Pilate.

64 AD: Great Fire of Rome occurs under the rule of Nero.

68-69 AD: Year of the Four Emperors. After Nero's death, Galba, Otho, Vitellius, and Vespasian all hold the title of Emperor in quick succession.

79 AD: Mount Vesuvius erupts, burying Pompeii and Herculaneum.

80 AD: Colosseum's construction is completed under Emperor Titus.

96-180 AD: The Five Good Emperors (Nerva, Trajan, Hadrian, Antoninus Pius, Marcus Aurelius) rule Rome, a period of peace, territorial expansion, and prosperity.

117 AD: Under Emperor Trajan, the Roman Empire reaches its greatest territorial extent.

180 AD: Death of Marcus Aurelius marks the end of the Pax Romana.

235-284 AD: Crisis of the Third Century. The Roman Empire experiences a period of chaos and decline characterized by civil wars, economic crisis, plague, and the dissolution of central power.

284 AD: Diocletian becomes Emperor, instigates numerous reforms to stabilize the empire, including dividing the empire into the Eastern and Western Roman Empires (Tetrarchy).

303 AD: Diocletian's "Great Persecution" against Christians in the Roman Empire begins.

312 AD: Battle of Milvian Bridge. Constantine I becomes Western Roman Emperor, begins to normalize Christianity.

313 AD: Edict of Milan. Constantine and Licinius agree to protect Christians in the Roman Empire.

325 AD: Council of Nicaea. The first council of Christian bishops, called by Constantine, results in the first uniform Christian doctrine, the Nicene Creed.

330 AD: Constantine moves the Roman capital to Byzantium, later renamed Constantinople.

395 AD: Death of Theodosius I, the last emperor to rule a united Roman Empire. The empire is permanently divided between his sons, Honorius (West) and Arcadius (East).

410 AD: Visigoths under King Alaric I sack Rome.

455 AD: Vandals, under King Genseric, sack Rome.

476 AD: Odoacer, a Germanic king, deposes Romulus Augustulus, the last Western Roman Emperor. The Fall of the Western Roman Empire is traditionally dated to this event.

527-565 AD: Reign of Justinian I. The Eastern Roman Empire (Byzantine Empire) reaches its greatest extent, temporarily reoccupying parts of the Western Empire, including Rome.

568 AD: Lombards invade Italy and establish a kingdom in the north.

800 AD: Charlemagne, king of the Franks, is crowned "Emperor of the Romans" by Pope Leo III, symbolizing the shift of Roman legacy to the Frankish lands and the beginning of what would later be known as the Holy Roman Empire.

1453 AD: Fall of Constantinople to the Ottoman Turks. This marks the end of the Eastern Roman Empire (Byzantine Empire), and is often used to mark the end of the Middle Ages in Europe.

FURTHER READING

Ando, C. (2000). Imperial Ideology and Provincial Loyalty in the Roman Empire. University of California Press.

Barnes, T. D. (1981). Constantine and Eusebius. Harvard University Press.

Birley, A. (1999). Septimius Severus: The African Emperor. Routledge.

Bowersock, G. W. (1978). Julian the Apostate. Harvard University Press.

Bowman, A. K., Cameron, A., & Garnsey, P. (2005). The Cambridge Ancient History: Volume 12, The Crisis of Empire, AD 193-337. Cambridge University Press.

Brown, P. (2013). The Rise of Western Christendom: Triumph and Diversity, A.D. 200-1000. Wiley-Blackwell.

Cameron, A. (1993). The Later Roman Empire: AD 284-430. Harvard University Press.

Campbell, B. (1994). The Roman Army, 31 B.C. - AD 337: A Sourcebook. Routledge.

Cary, M., & Scullard, H. H. (1975). A History of Rome. Palgrave Macmillan.

Demandt, A. (1984). Der Fall Roms: Die Auflösung des römischen Reiches im Urteil der Nachwelt. C.H. Beck.

Drummond, A. (1995). Law, Politics and Power: Sallust and the Execution of the Catilinarian Conspirators. Historia: Zeitschrift für Alte Geschichte, 1995.

Elton, H. (1998). Warfare in Roman Europe, AD 350-425. Oxford University Press.

Fagan, G. (2002). Bathing in Public in the Roman World. University of Michigan Press.

Ferrill, A. (1988). The Fall of the Roman Empire: The Military Explanation. Thames & Hudson.

Gibbon, E. (2003). The Decline and Fall of the Roman Empire. Penguin Classics.

Goldsworthy, A. (2010). How Rome Fell: Death of a Superpower. Yale University Press.

Grant, M. (1999). The Collapse and Recovery of the Roman Empire. Routledge.

Heather, P. (2010). Empires and Barbarians: The Fall of Rome and the Birth of Europe. Oxford University Press.

Heather, P. (2007). The Fall of the Roman Empire: A New History of Rome and the Barbarians. Oxford University Press.

Heather, P. (2014). The Restoration of Rome: Barbarian Popes and Imperial Pretenders. Oxford University Press.

Holmes, G. (2001). The Oxford History of Medieval Europe. Oxford University Press.

Jones, A. H. M. (1986). The Later Roman Empire, 284-602: A Social, Economic, and Administrative Survey. The Johns Hopkins University Press.

Kelly, C. (2006). The Roman Empire: A Very Short Introduction. Oxford University Press.

Luttwak, E. N. (1979). The Grand Strategy of the Roman Empire: From the First Century C.E. to the Third. The Johns Hopkins University Press.

MacMullen, R. (1986). Christianizing the Roman Empire: (A.D. 100-400). Yale University Press.

Matyszak, P. (2004). The Enemies of Rome: From Hannibal to Attila the Hun. Thames & Hudson.

Millar, F. (1993). The Roman Near East, 31 B.C.–A.D. 337. Harvard University Press

Mommsen, T. (2017). The History of Rome. CreateSpace Independent Publishing Platform.

Nixey, C. (2018). The Darkening Age: The Christian Destruction of the Classical World. Houghton Mifflin Harcourt.

Potter, D. S. (2004). The Roman Empire at Bay, AD 180-395. Routledge.

Potter, D. (2015). Theodora: Actress, Empress, Saint. Oxford University Press.

Raaflaub, K. A. (2007). War and Peace in the Ancient World. Wiley-Blackwell.

Roberts, J. (2007). The Oxford Dictionary of the Classical World. Oxford University Press.

Rostovtzeff, M. (1957). The Social and Economic History of the Roman Empire. Biblo & Tannen Publishers.

Scarre, C. (1995). Chronicle of the Roman Emperors: The Reign-by-Reign Record of the Rulers of Imperial Rome. Thames & Hudson.

Sear, D. R. (2000). Roman Coins and Their Values, Vol I: The Republic and The Twelve Caesars 280 BC-AD 96. Spink & Son Ltd.

Southern, P. (2001). The Roman Empire from Severus to Constantine. Routledge.

Starr, C. G. (1991). A History of the Ancient World. Oxford University Press.

Syme, R. (2002). The Roman Revolution. Oxford University Press.

Tainter, J. A. (1988). The Collapse of Complex Societies. Cambridge University Press.

Treadgold, W. (1997). A History of the Byzantine State and Society. Stanford University Press.

Ward-Perkins, B. (2006). The Fall of Rome: And the End of Civilization. Oxford University Press.

Watson, G. R. (1969). The Roman Soldier. Cornell University Press.

Wells, C. (1992). The Roman Empire. Harvard University Press.

Williams, S. (1997). Diocletian and the Roman Recovery. Routledge.

Woolf, G. (2012). Rome: An Empire's Story. Oxford University Press.

Made in the USA
Las Vegas, NV
15 December 2023

82909903R00062